THIS BOOK IS LOVINGLY DEDICATED TO MY MOTHER

Funeral Poems And Reflections — Volume I

Contents

Memorial Poems For Everyone

Memorial Poems For Family

FUNERAL POEMS AND REFLECTIONS — VOLUME I
CONTENTS

MEMORIAL POEMS FOR FAMILY MEMBERS

Funeral Poems And Reflections — Volume I

Contents

Memorial Poems For Family Members

Other Memorial Poems

Funeral Poems And Reflections — Volume I
Contents

Other Memorial Poems

Permissions And Use

-The purchaser of this book has the right to replicate the poem(s) contained in the book on a funeral or memorial program to share with mourners.

-Minor changes to the poem(s) in vocal, or written, format are allowed, such as changing the words "I" and "We".

-The poem(s) in this book may not be mass emailed, or replicated either electronically, vocally, or in print format for mass distribution. Doing so is a violation of the author's copyright rights. [For example: The poem(s) cannot be placed on online memorial websites.]

-Many poems have a Line symbol in them: —. This line (—) is a cue to take a longer pause when reading the poem orally.

-Use of these poems for charitable, or business, purposes without written permission of the author is prohibited.

-Additional funeral and memorial poems and quotes are available at: WWW.FUNERALPOEMSANDREFLECTIONS.COM

-Any special requests to use the poem(s) outside the boundaries of personal use, or for use as epitaphs, must be approved by the author, Jilchristy Dee, in writing.

-The author can be reached via email at: JILCHRISTY@FUNERALPOEMSANDREFLECTIONS.COM

Funeral Poems And Reflections

Volume I

A Prayer For Understanding

Dear Lord as we now gather near
To mourn the one we love
Bestow Your understanding here
Your peace from up above

Please heal our hearts
It hurts so much
That we must say goodbye!
Support us through these dark, sad hours
As we remember, grieve and cry

Although we cannot understand
We pray we'll someday know
Why you took (Loved One's Name) away from us
Back to Your heavenly home

Give us Your strength
And help us through
The days and years to come
May sweet mem'ries warm our hearts and minds
Like golden rays of sun

Please let (Loved One's Name) stay close nearby
To watch over us we plead
A guardian angel's support from heaven
Whenever we have need

Surround us with Your love and hope
And console us in our grief
May bitter sorrow be lessened 'til
It becomes accepting peace

And may we be reunited soon
One day...never again to part
With (Loved One's Name) that we hold so very dear
And grieve now in our hearts

We'll Remember You

We'll remember you in sunshine
Its rays warming earth and sky
We'll remember you in birds' graceful wings
As they glide and flutter by

We'll remember you in the summer breeze
And in softly falling rain
We'll remember you in dark storm clouds
The rainbow's picture frame

We'll remember you in blossoms and fields
And in gentle streams that flow
We'll remember you in all that lives...
All that brings life...that grows

We'll remember you in the mountains
When golden leaves fall at our feet
We'll remember you when glowing sunsets
Cast sparkling embers on the beach

We'll remember you in the Christmas lights
Glimmering bright with joy and hope
We'll remember you when white winter storms
Cover canyon, field and slope

We'll remember you when we're at our best
Keep your mem'ry close during darkest days
We'll remember you when each day dawns
In these simple, yet precious ways

Moment by moment we'll remember you
You'll never be too far away
Because we'll keep you in our hearts
Each and every day

Celebrating You

Dear (Loved One's Name) we're all assembled
We've come to honor you
To share sweet recollections
And express our gratitude

You were a great example
Of the best way one can live
Your generous, loving spirit
Was a daily gift you chose to give

And we knew that we were privileged
To know someone so dear
You shared our lives, both the good and bad
Our true friend throughout the years

You took each day and challenge
Exactly as it came
Your spirit remained steadfast
Life couldn't make you change

Quite often we would marvel
At the determination found in you
How much we'll miss your courage
And your fearless attitude!

Still we know that you'll continue
To be the incredible soul you are
And though we cannot see you
We trust you'll never be far

Because a soul so special
Can never truly go away
You'll always be an inspiration
Blessing our lives each day

So as we bid you farewell...for now
It's with deepest love and gratitude
Counting our lives quite blessed to have known
Someone As Wonderful As You
Alt. Verse: A friend/sister/brother, etc. as wonderful as you

Takin' The Train To Heaven

Heaven's train has come 'a callin'
The conductor tells me "time to go"
I hadn't seen it comin'
I wish that I'd 'a known

Soft smoke is billowin', billowin' up
The train whistles a fluted sound
And up eternity's track we go
Leavin' this earthly ground

I'd like to have known my passage was booked
The fare paid...my departure planned
'Cause I was just as surprised as you
When from life-to-death I spanned

So here I stand on the departure docks
And into eternity I'll go
But I'll leave part of my heart with you
So you will always know...

THAT I LOVE YOU

—

I've found my seat now on the train
It's feelin' more like home
As for baggage, we all have none
C'ept for love n' memories we've known

My ticket's punched and handed back
After searchin' my heart and face
I find it reads: "FIRST CLASS TO HEAVEN"
"THROUGH CHRIST'S ATONING GRACE"

T<small>AKIN</small>' T<small>HE</small> T<small>RAIN</small> T<small>O</small> H<small>EAVEN</small> (C<small>ONTINUED</small>)

A<small>ND SUDDENLY</small> I'<small>M FEELIN</small>' <small>SO MUCH CALM</small>
'B<small>OUT WHERE</small> I'<small>VE BEEN AND WHERE</small> I'<small>M GOIN</small>'
A<small>ND</small> I <small>CAN TRUST YOU ALL TO</small> G<small>OD</small>'<small>S SWEET GRACE</small>
F<small>OR HIS MERCIES YOU</small>'<small>LL BE KNOWIN</small>'

I <small>CAN SEE YOU ALL SO CLEARLY</small>
A<small>S THE TRAIN CHUGS N</small>' <small>WE DEPART</small>
Y<small>OU</small>'<small>RE ALL REMAININ</small>' <small>SO CLOSE TO ME</small>
W<small>HERE DOES</small> L<small>IFE END N</small>' H<small>EAVEN START</small>?

I <small>STILL CAN REACH OUT N</small>' <small>TOUCH YOU</small>
S<small>O</small> I'<small>LL BE SENDIN</small>' <small>MY LOVE EACH DAY</small>
Y<small>OUR SORROW</small>'<small>S GONNA EASE WITH TIME</small>
Y<small>ET MY HEARTFELT LOVE WILL ALWAYS STAY</small>

—

T<small>HE TRAIN BEGINS TO SLOW DOWN NOW</small>...
W<small>E</small>'<small>RE ARRIVIN</small>' <small>AT ETERNITY</small>
A<small>S HEAV</small>'<small>NLY MANSIONS COME INTO VIEW</small>...
G<small>LORIOUS AS THEY CAN BE</small>!

S<small>O DON</small>'<small>T BE FILLED WITH SADNESS</small>!
I'<small>M WITH</small> G<small>OD NOW YOU SEE</small>...
A<small>WAITIN</small>' <small>THE DAY WHEN</small> Y<small>OU</small>'<small>LL TAKE THE TRAIN</small>...
W<small>HEN YOU</small>'<small>LL RETURN AGAIN TO ME</small>

You Left At Sunset

You left at sunset
My heart was filled with sorrow
Wishing for more time with you
Knowing every moment with you
Had been a precious gift

You brought me joy
Infused my life with happiness
Filled my heart with peace
And warmed me with your love

It wasn't until after you'd parted
That I realized you left at sunset
For the earth and sky were still bathed
In shining rays of rose-gold light

And there was a tangible peace in the air
A sweet and beautiful calm
And I could feel it touch the depth of sadness
That had opened in my heart

It seemed that the whole earth was reminding me
That the privilege of knowing you
Far outweighed the sadness of a goodbye

And as the sun continued its course, beyond my view
I thought of what a fitting tribute it was
That you left at the most glorious moment of the day
When the earth and heavens are transformed in brilliance

How perfectly fitting...
Because knowing you transformed me
Just like the sun, you brought more life
More warmth and more joy into my heart
You touched my soul in a life-affirming and beautiful way

You Left At Sunset (Continued)

Now like the sun moving over the horizon
You've moved to a place beyond my sight
But I know you haven't disappeared
Your spirit's still shining in heavenly realms

That just as the sun was setting here
Others were experiencing a glorious dawn
Basking in the light of your unforgettable spirit
Being touched by the sweet essence of you

I will miss you more than you will ever know
You were a cherished presence
And I will think of you every day
I'll honor your loss through sweet memories
Your influence will stay with me forever

And just as we experience a tug and a longing
When the setting sun spreads golden rays throughout the sky
I'll remember you too with longing...and a smile
Feeling eternally grateful to have known you

Before you left at sunset...
And moved forward in the dawn...

We Didn't Get To Say Goodbye

We didn't get to say goodbye
We're devastated that you're gone
We'd have done anything to keep you here with us
Right here where you belong

We didn't know that life would take
Such an unexpected path
That you'd be separated from us so soon
Heartbreaking reality we struggle to grasp

And bitter though our losing you has been
And so profound is the pain we bear
We're sadder still at no chance for goodbye
No final expression of our deep love and care

Yet believing that you're not too far away
That your Spirit still lingers quite near
We'll say our goodbyes in our words and our thoughts
Trusting that each one you'll hear

First know that you are loved in the truest of ways
So deep that only our hearts can give expression
And you'll be forever surrounded by our love
For we're sending it straight up to Heaven

Please know that you'll be cherished by each of us
For your example and kindness we'll treasure
We understand now how your life was a gift
That was meant to bless us forever

And though we'll miss you terribly
We want your Spirit to be free
Free to enjoy all the wonders of Heaven
Not bound to us in our grief

<u>We Didn't Get To Say Goodbye (Continued)</u>

So watch over us with happiness from Heaven
For we'll remember you with mem'ries so sweet
And we'll bravely endure till you're with us again
When our hearts will be healed and complete

For surely one day we'll be together again
In God's arms and in Heaven with you
For death cannot conquer a love that's as strong
As the love that we all feel for you

I'M FREE

Don't mourn for me, I'm free
The struggle is finally finished
My spirit's free, my body's at rest
Yet I am not diminished

I've simply moved to that heavenly phase
Of God's almighty plan
Having completed the trials of life
In heaven's peace is where I stand

Untouched by the pain that assailed my body
Unaffected by the illness' rage
Grateful the struggle is finally over
That I've moved beyond such a difficult stage

Now surrounded by my loved ones who've passed
Being joyfully reunited with them
Watching over you with deepest love and affection
From the serenity and peace found in heaven

And I'm grateful for a love that deepened
As you patiently cared for me
Love so strong...I didn't think it could be expanded
Yet it grew more tender 'midst such suffering and grief

Now death has required that I leave you for a time
Abiding in a place of beauty you can't yet see
For 'tis not your time to come back to heaven
But someday you'll return to be with me

Till then, accept the peace that I'm not suffering
That I've been released from relentless misery
From an illness that overtook my body
Till only death could provide a release

I'm Free (Continued)

Yet my spirit was never conquered
I live on and I'll watch over you
At times you'll feel my love and presence
When you need my support to be with you

So don't mourn me for long, nor too profoundly
For I haven't gone far, you'll see
Be happy I'm not trapped in a broken body
Rejoice that my spirit's now free

A Cherished Mother And Grandmother

A cherished Mother and Grandmother
You are and were, and will forever be
You loved us throughout a lifetime
And we'll love you throughout eternity

As children, your were our Mom and our strength
The force upon which we relied
You helped us grow through life's laughter and tears
And you always stood by our side

You were so strong and worked so hard
To take good care of us
Hours spent...such time we can't comprehend!
Proved your faithful devotion to us

And when we brought our own children home
Your commitment only grew
You helped them, played with, and loved them
As only a Grandmother can do

And our children...they came to adore you!
For you spoiled them with love and affection
You treasured each one in such special ways
There are too many examples to mention

And though they were denied more days and years
With a Grandmother as wonderful as you
You've filled their hearts with sweet memories
That'll remain a whole lifetime through

A Cherished Mother And Grandmother (Continued)

—

Dearest Mother and Grandmother, we love you!
We find we cannot do enough
To express the depths of our gratitude
For your sacrifice and your love

But trust that you'll be remembered
In sweetest memories every day
For you have blessed our lives forever
Through your goodness, love and strength!

Nana

It's never easy to say goodbye
"Nana's gone" was difficult to hear
It's hard to find the right words to say
For our Nana was so dear!

She loved us...deeply loved us
With her strong, maternal pride
We were always safe and happy
With Nana by our side

She wasn't simply "Grandma"
That word does not suffice
To express our love for Nana
Who was so important to our lives

Nana would always help us
She'd give most anything
To see that we were happy
And living out our dreams

We loved to be with Nana
In truth, she spoiled us
Through her loving affection
Nana came to mean so much

For she took the time to spend with us
That few would ever do
She'd be with us, share with us and play with us
Until we'd exhausted her through

But never once did we begin to doubt
That she'd return again
A little rest and she was back
Our true and faithful friend

NANA (CONTINUED)

NOW, NANA WASN'T ALWAYS GENTLE
IN FACT, SHE COULD BE STERN
SHE HAD HIGH EXPECTATIONS OF US
WHICH WE QUICKLY CAME TO LEARN

BUT EVEN WHILE SHE WAS BEING STRICT
DEEP DOWN INSIDE WE ALWAYS KNEW
SHE ONLY WANTED THE BEST FOR US
AND OUR LOVE FOR HER? IT GREW!

—

NANA, YOU WERE SO SPECIAL
YOU CAPTURED ALL OUR HEARTS
AND THOUGH YOU'RE NO LONGER WITH US
YOUR INFLUENCE WILL NEVER PART

YOU WERE WITH US FROM THE BEGINNING
AND WE LOVED YOU MORE EACH DAY
YOU'LL NEVER BE GONE FROM US NANA
FOR IN OUR HEARTS YOU'LL ALWAYS STAY

Grandpa Is Coming For Grandma

Grandpa is coming for Grandma
We all know it...we all feel it
Just as the sun can be felt through a window pane
Grandpa's presence comes here time and time again

Day by day he comes
And he lingers by her side
He waits for death to claim her
When heartbeat and breath subside

Grandpa sees her fight the battle
We all know she just can't win
And tells her to be brave and strong
She'll soon be with him again

He gently takes her hand in his
The softest of touches he makes
Grandpa's spirit gently caresses her skin
When he touches his sweetheart's face

And on occasion Grandma feels him now
How wonderful it seems!
A moment's rest through this battle stage
Like a sweet and beautiful dream

And for one brief moment she forgets her pain
And feels much like a young, new bride
She yearns to see Grandpa's face again
To never leave his side

So while we wait through days and hours
Till the dreaded goodbye must come
Grandpa waits with growing excitement
He's been without her far too long

Grandpa Is Coming For Grandma (Continued)

Grandpa understands the sorrow we feel
For we also once mourned him in grief
He stands by our side to lend us support
And hopes we'll find comfort and peace

He wants us to know that he is okay
And Grandma will soon be too
Death's separation didn't diminish their love
Through years of longing...it only grew
Alt. Verse: Through deepest longing...it only grew

And so with each breath as we see Grandma
Lose her grasp on this life she's known
She's moving closer towards Grandpa
For he's come to take her home...

—

And when that final, sacred moment came
Grandma slipped just beyond our grasp
And Grandpa embraced her with open arms
Welcoming her home at last

So for all in th'hereafter we don't understand
Yet hope someday to know
We are certain Grandma is safe and well
For Grandpa came and carried her home

We Love And Honor You Grandma

We love and honor you Grandma
With all our hearts...Forever
You are a part of our happiness
Cherished and respected

Our esteem for you...
It grew throughout our lives
Your love wasn't valued for love's sake alone
To us, this love has become your legacy

It has transcended the life you lived
And has not only filled our hearts with happy memories
But also has encouraged us to be better
To be more like the type of person you were

A person of love and kindness
A true friend
Caring and compassionate
Loyal beyond words

We love you Grandma
With all our hearts...Forever
For supporting us
Encouraging us
Balancing the truth you spoke
With the love you felt
So that we were both improved and guided
Through your enduring presence
And patient, loving example

We respect you Grandma
And we'll endeavor to honor you
Not only through our words
But also through our deeds

WE LOVE AND HONOR YOU GRANDMA (CONTINUED)

MEEKLY TRYING TO ACHIEVE THE MEASURE OF THE PERSON YOU WERE
AND HOPING OUR ATTEMPTS WILL BRING YOU PRIDE AND SATISFACTION
FROM YOUR RIGHTFUL VANTAGE POINT IN HEAVEN

FOR WE LOVE YOU GRANDMA
AND WE WANT TO HONOR YOU
FOREVER

What Makes A Grandmother Special

What makes a Grandmother special?
Why is she so dear?
When we think about our Grandma
The reasons are quite clear

Our Grandma loved us dearly
We could see it every time
We came to visit Grandma
In the way her eyes would shine

And we could tell that she was happy
When we were with her
She'd laugh and play and hug us
These sweet memories will endure!

Grandma was known to spoil us
For she knew just what we liked
She paid attention to the things we'd say
And helped our dreams take flight

She always listened closely
Had such a tender and loving gaze
Doted on us with her smiles and hugs
And her kind and thoughtful ways

So what made our Grandma special?
So special, she stood apart?
It's that she showered our lives with such deep love
That she'll live forever in our hearts

Our Grandpa

We had the greatest Grandpa
Not a stuffy, distant one
His hair reflected shades of gray
But his spirit was bright and young

We knew he always loved us
For his smile was easily found
Mirrored in his twinkling eyes
Whenever we were around

We always appreciated
All the special things he did
His loving, kind expressions
And the honorable way he lived

But most of all we always felt
His unconditional love
Grandpa, please know we loved you too
So very, very much!

When we think about our Grandpa
We know we couldn't have hoped for more
Than the love we had from Grandpa
Whom we cherished and adored!

Special Times With Grandpa

As I think back on time with Grandpa
So many memories come to mind
But one theme stays consistent
They were filled with special times

From camping in the mountains
And being on the water
To reeling in the "big one"
And struggling till we caught 'er

Grandpa took the time to be there
At childhood events and on special days
I'd search his face out in the crowd
Until I'd found his gaze

And I loved to hear him cheer me on
To see his look of pride
As I tried my very best
To reach my goals in life

Grandpa was a trusted advisor
Equipped with the wisdom of age
Who helped me sort out the choices
On the path my life would take

And when we'd talk, he'd share his life
Then the years just seemed to melt
And he didn't seem too different from me
When he was younger, like myself

Special Times With Grandpa (Continued)

So through the years, Grandpa has been there
To love and cheer and care
Filling my life with special moments
That we two were privileged to share

And I'll be forever grateful
For the love he gave to me
My Grandpa will live on forever
In my heart and memory

WE LOVE AND HONOR YOU GRANDPA

We love and honor you Grandpa
With all our hearts...Forever
You are a part of our happiness
Cherished and respected

Our esteem for you...
It grew throughout our lives
Your love wasn't valued for love's sake alone
To us, this love has become your legacy

It has transcended the life you lived
And has not only filled our hearts with happy memories
But also has encouraged us to be better
To be more like the type of person you were

A person of love and kindness
A true friend
Caring and compassionate
Loyal beyond words

We love you Grandpa
With all our hearts...Forever
For supporting us
Encouraging us
Balancing the truth you spoke
With the love you felt
So that we were both improved and protected
Through your enduring presence
And patient, loving example

We respect you Grandpa
And we'll endeavor to honor you
Not only through our words
But also through our deeds

We Love And Honor You Grandpa (Continued)

Meekly trying to achieve the measure of the person you were
And hoping our attempts will bring you pride and satisfaction
From your rightful vantage point in heaven

For we love you Grandpa
And we want to honor you
Forever

THERE SHOULD HAVE BEEN MORE ROSES

THERE SHOULD HAVE BEEN MORE "THANK YOU'S"
MANY MORE "I LOVE YOU'S"
MORE TIME FOR SPECIAL MOMENTS
AND A FEW MORE ROSES TOO

LIFE JUST SEEMED TO TAKE ITS COURSE
AND THOUGH IT WAS NEVER INTENDED
YOU WERE NOT CHERISHED, AS YOU SHOULD HAVE BEEN
AND NOW IT CAN'T BE MENDED

FOR THERE, LEFT FORGOTTEN, IN THE DAY-TO-DAY
(THOUGH THAT SHOULDN'T BE AN EXCUSE)
WERE SO MANY OPPORTUNITIES LOST
TO EXPRESS LOVE AND GRATITUDE

FOR EVERYTHING YOU DID EACH DAY
FOR THE DEDICATION THAT IT TOOK
TO KEEP ON GOING IN SPITE OF THE FACT
THAT YOUR EFFORTS WERE OFTEN OVERLOOKED

AND IT'S A PAINFUL THING TO CONSIDER THIS
TO WISH THE PAST COULD SOMEHOW BE CHANGED
AND TO BE HAUNTED BY THE REALIZATION
THAT THIS CAN NEVER BE ARRANGED

—

PLEASE KNOW YOU'LL BE REMEMBERED FOREVER
FOR ALL THE WONDERFUL THINGS YOU DID
AND MISSED MOST OF ALL FOR THE LOVE YOU SHOWED
THROUGH COUNTLESS WAYS EV'RY DAY THAT YOU LIVED

There Should Have Been More Roses (Continued)

And these feeble words are meant to express
Heartfelt love, with an apology of regret
Realizing that you were never cherished
As you truly should have been

With deepest longing that will last forever
Understanding the gratitude you should have been due
And wishing that you were still here to receive
A few more roses too

I'll Remember You

I'll remember you in sunshine
Its rays warming earth and sky
I'll remember you in birds' graceful wings
As they glide and flutter by

I'll remember you in the summer breeze
And in softly falling rain
I'll remember you in dark storm clouds
The rainbow's picture frame

I'll remember you in blossoms and fields
And in gentle streams that flow
I'll remember you in all that lives...
All that brings life...that grows

I'll remember you in the mountains
When golden leaves fall at my feet
I'll remember you when glowing sunsets
Cast sparkling embers on the beach

I'll remember you in the Christmas lights
Glimmering bright with joy and hope
I'll remember you when white winter storms
Cover canyon, field and slope

I'll remember you in all my heartbeats
Which steadily and softly beat
I'll remember, because without you, Love
I wouldn't be complete

I'll Remember You (Continued)

I'll remember you when I'm at my best
Keep your mem'ry close during darkest days
I'll remember you when each day dawns
In these simple, yet precious ways

Moment by moment I'll remember you
You'll never be too far away
Because I'll keep you in my heart
Each and every day

A Wife As Wonderful As You

I love you dearly, with all my heart
My cherished wife and friend
Ours is a love that deepened through the years
And it's a love that will never end

Thank you for being the kind of wife and mother
Who blessed our home and family
By doing special things for each one of us
And loving us unconditionally

You watched over us in good times and bad
You honored every wedding vow
As you cared for us in sickness and health
And we feel lost without you now

It's so hard to realize that life has changed
And it will never be the same again
As I face a lonelier future
Without you, my dearest wife and friend

I can only feel to honor you
And to be grateful for all the memories
That you lovingly created throughout the years
Memories, which mean everything to me

And even though I'll miss you every day
I still promise to try my best
To fill the gap...the immeasurable gap
In our family that your passing left

And I'll honor you forever, (Wife's Name)
With expressions of love and gratitude
Understanding how very blessed I was
To have a wife as wonderful as you

Dearest Husband

Dearest Husband, I thank you with all of my heart
For sharing this journey called life
I'll be forever grateful
That I was blessed to be your wife

Grateful to have held your hand
To have loved you throughout the years
Amidst life's joys and challenges
In times of happiness and tears

Blessed to have built a life with you
To have created a family
For our love, and that of our children
alt. verse: For our love, and that of our son/daughter
Means everything to me

I can hardly accept you've been taken away
I can hardly bear the thought
Of facing the future without you here
I'm still not sure how I'll get through this loss

Yet I'm comforted knowing how much you love us
And I'm certain you're still watching o'er
Staying nearby and caring for us
As faithfully as before

And though you may be gone for a season
I'll carry on...trusting to see you again
Waiting 'til God reunites us in heaven
And brings me back to you, sweetheart and friend

Until then...I thank you, dearest husband
For all you've meant to my life
I'm so grateful God made us a family
And for the blessing of being your wife

A Determined Mother

The life of a child she carefully shapes
From her child's first breath
She understands the power
Of the legacy she must leave

She is responsible for raising a child after all
It is with a solemn joy that she accepts this task

The love she feels for her child cannot be explained
It runs too deep, fills her soul with too much joy
And is simply too beautiful to be described by mere words

She understands her privilege
And accepts the gift of motherhood
With a firm, determined commitment
She will raise a child to be proud of...

The years are long and trying
Yet on special, unexpected occasions
She is rewarded with a brief glimpse
Of the difference she is making

Every experience, she understands
Can be a lesson, a test or a gift
For her precious child

And she prepares her child dutifully
And lovingly...
For she is a Determined Mother

She lives daily with integrity
An example of hard work and love
Her child recognizes her goodness
And desires to follow her footsteps

A Determined Mother (Continued)

In time the child learns how to travel through life
How to accept both the good and the bad
And is grateful for the profound example
Of one Determined Mother

And when this Mother has departed
The world is better because she came
For her legacy is firmly planted
In the precious child she raised

HE IS COMING FOR HER

HE IS COMING FOR HER
WE ALL KNOW IT...WE ALL FEEL IT
JUST AS THE SUN CAN BE FELT THROUGH A WINDOW PANE
DAD'S PRESENCE COMES HERE TIME AND TIME AGAIN

DAY BY DAY HE COMES
AND HE LINGERS BY HER SIDE
HE WAITS FOR DEATH TO CLAIM HER
WHEN HEARTBEAT AND BREATH SUBSIDE

HE SEES HER FIGHT THE BATTLE
WE KNOW SHE JUST CAN'T WIN
AND TELLS HER TO BE BRAVE AND STRONG
SHE'LL SOON BE WITH HIM AGAIN

HE GENTLY TAKES HER HAND IN HIS
THE SOFTEST OF TOUCHES HE MAKES
DAD'S SPIRIT GENTLY CARESSES HER SKIN
WHEN HE TOUCHES HIS SWEETHEART'S FACE

ON OCCASION SHE CAN FEEL HIM NOW
HOW WONDERFUL IT SEEMS!
A MOMENT'S REST THROUGH THIS BATTLE STAGE
LIKE A SWEET AND BEAUTIFUL DREAM

AND FOR ONE BRIEF MOMENT SHE FORGETS HER PAIN
AND FEELS MUCH LIKE A YOUNG, NEW BRIDE
SHE YEARNS TO SEE HER HUSBAND'S FACE AGAIN
TO NEVER LEAVE HIS SIDE

SO WHILE WE WAIT THROUGH DAYS AND HOURS
TILL THE DREADED GOODBYE MUST COME
DAD WAITS WITH GROWING EXCITEMENT
HE'S BEEN WITHOUT HER FAR TOO LONG

He Is Coming For Her (Continued)

Dad understands the sorrow we feel
For we also once mourned him in grief
He stands by our side to lend us support
And hopes we'll find comfort and peace

He wants us to know that he is okay
And Mom will soon be too
Death's separation didn't diminish their love
Through years of longing...it only grew
Alt. Verse: Through deepest longing...it only grew

And so with each breath as we see our Mom
Lose her grasp on this life she's known
She's moving closer and closer to Dad
For he's come to take her home...

—

And when that final, sacred moment came
Mom slipped just beyond our grasp
And Dad embraced her with open arms
Welcoming her home at last

So for all in th'hereafter we don't understand
Yet hope someday to know
We are certain Mom is safe and well
'Cause Dad came and carried her home

A Tribute To My Mother

My Mother...
She was my shining example
Of strength and compassion
And of honor and love

I was grateful to call her "Mom"
She made me proud
She wasn't only my Mother
She was my dear friend

My Mother had great strength
And she was wise...
I always knew I could draw from her strength
Whenever I needed it
It gave me courage to grow up and take risks
To experience life's successes...
And a few of its failures

Mother's compassion for others was so deep!
She looked for the need and she filled it
She treated others with kindness and respect
And many lives were blessed through her goodness

Mother was an honorable woman
This wasn't just a mere aspect of her personality
It was the very foundation of her character
It's impossible to think of Mom
without such words as honor, dignity and respect
Quickly coming to mind

But most of all...Mother was love

I am convinced that the world
will never be as bright and beautiful
As it was when my Mother was here

A Tribute To My Mother (Continued)

Mom's love was unconditional
And the sweetest and most enduring part of her love is
That it will always be with me
It was my Mother's most important...and final gift to me

To my dear Mother... I have a few pledges to make to you
First- I'll try to make you proud every day
Second- Even though I'll miss you terribly
I promise to bravely face the coming days
I also promise to be happy
Not to dwell in sadness too long
Without recalling the wonderful memories
You've filled my life with

Most of all....
I promise to try to pattern my life more after yours

For there could be no more fitting tribute
To ever reach my ears
Than to be referred to as..."My Mother's Daughter"
alternate ending: "My Mother's Son"

Your Dreams Were All For Us Mom

Your dreams were all for us Mom, all for us
You traded your own dreams to purchase ours
Willing to accept lesser opportunities
So that we would have every opportunity

Every possibility
Every chance for a good education
Every security and confidence
Everything!

And our dreams became your hopes and aspirations
We knew that we were never alone in our dreams
For you were right there with us

You didn't mind if you didn't get the best education
As long as we were afforded that opportunity
It didn't matter if your work wasn't what you had hoped for
As long as it gave us the means to create our own futures

You willingly accepted all those hours away from us
Working long and hard
You were okay with it...
As long as it provided your family with security and stability
So we grew up surrounded in your deep love and in your safety
You provided the room in our hearts for imagination to grow
You took care of the worries
So that our hearts and minds could pursue our dreams

You never spent much on yourself
You never enjoyed many of the finer things in life
We were the treasure you invested your life in
And you gave everything you had for us
Everything Mom!
Everything!

Your Dreams Were All For Us Mom (Continued)

And now we have lives that are abundant and full
Blessed with rich memories and cherished opportunities
We are surrounded in the peace and love of family
And trusted, loyal friends

We have a life that was paid for in advance
Through the difficult and dedicated efforts of a loving mother
Who traded the best years of her own life
To make sure we'd have the best years of ours

Mom, you will never be forgotten!
Your love and sacrifice will never leave us
We will never question our own true worth
For you proved our value to us every single day

And now we hope that our lives have rewarded <u>your</u> dreams
Satisfied every dedicated effort you gave for us
Given you every honor
Every sense of pride
Every happiness and peace
Every dream fulfilled
Everything!

You and your cherished legacy will live on forever
In the lives and hearts of your family
For you have truly purchased a better life for all of us
Through everything that you willingly sacrificed
You gave us everything Mom!
Everything!

A Mother's Touch

A mother's touch is a gentle caress
As she welcomes her children to life
Arms outstretched to hold each new "bundle"
While her newborns are laid by her side

A mother's touch is a promise kept
To care for her children's every need
Hands feeding, changing and bathing
The precious babes she rocks to sleep

And a mother's touch continues to bless
Through the toddler and childhood days
Ever guiding and tenderly serving
The children she's privileged to raise

Steadying bikes while they learn to ride
Baking warm cookies and treats
Bandaging the wounds of playtime adventures
All things that make childhood complete

And if her children are sick...they cry out for her
Longing for the comfort of her touch
Wanting nothing more than to be held in her arms
Trusting the healing power of her love

And as they grow, their needs often change
But their need for her never does
No child ever outgrows the need for a loving mother
Or the reassuring comfort of her touch

—

A Mother's Touch (Continued)

And when a loving mother has left this earth
Her children continue her pattern of care and patience
And ultimately her tender devotion becomes
A legacy carried onward to future generations

Together Again

A reunion occurred in heaven this week
Of the sweetest and most joyful kind
As Dad's spirit moved beyond this earth
Alt. Verse: As Mom's spirit moved beyond this earth
Released from his mortal life
Alt. Verse: Released from her mortal life

And what a reunion it must have been!
A joy beyond our conceiving
When Dad met Mom in heaven again
Alt. Verse: When Mom met Dad in heaven again
Ending years of dignified grieving

And we are certain Dad is still holding Mom's hand
While she cherishes each moment by his side
And they're experiencing the joy of being together again
Catching up on the years they were denied

We are confident they are also looking over us
Hoping this happiness will lessen our pain
As we contemplate the joy that they finally feel
Now that they are together again

And though we'll miss them terribly
And will long for them with deepest grief
We are reminded that love is more powerful than death
And this knowledge gives us comfort and peace

We can still feel their love surround us
Giving us a desire to continue on
To try our best to live our lives well
In the ways they would have done

TOGETHER AGAIN (CONTINUED)

FOR WE KNOW THIS ISN'T THE ONLY REUNION
SOMEDAY WE'LL BE CALLED BACK TO BE WITH THEM
FOR LIFE CAN LEAD US TO GREATER HAPPINESS
WITH THE LORD AND OUR LOVED ONES IN HEAVEN

—

SO ALTHOUGH WE'LL MISS OUR DAD PROFOUNDLY
ALT. VERSE: SO ALTHOUGH WE'LL MISS OUR MOM PROFOUNDLY
OUR GRIEF IS SOMEWHAT LESSENED
FOR WE ARE COMFORTED KNOWING THAT HE LED A GOOD LIFE
ALT. VERSE: FOR WE ARE COMFORTED THAT SHE LED A GOOD LIFE
AND IS NOW WITH MOM IN HEAVEN
ALT. VERSE: AND IS NOW WITH DAD IN HEAVEN

To The One Who Loved And Raised Me

*Note: This is a funeral poem for an adoptive parent,
Grandparent, Guardian or foster parent

To the one who loved and raised me
And cared for me as your own
Willing to give up an easier life
To bring me into your home

Who let me know that I was important
And definitely worth the time
That others would not...or could not give
After too many promises left behind

And I was deeply grateful
To finally have a home
That seemed to have a place for me
That I could call my own

And my love for you, it grew daily
And my trust seemed easier to share
As I opened myself up in a way
That in the past I wouldn't have dared

You gave me a lifetime of happy mem'ries
That slowly erased the bad
Instilling in me a hope for the future
That before, I'd never had

So as I say goodbye and remember you
It's with deepest gratitude to God above
For you were the angel He sent into my life
Who blessed me with your protection and your love

Dear Dad

Not many people have a father like you
We were one of the lucky few
We always knew how much we were loved
For you showed it in all you'd do

Growing up you took the time
To do the special things
That every child would hope to do
Fulfilling our childhood dreams

We always knew we could count on you
That for us you'd always be there
It helped us to grow up secure
Confident in your love and care

And as we started to get older
We weren't the easiest kids to raise
Your patience through our rebellious years
Still leaves us humbled and amazed

And over time we've continued to learn
All the lessons you had to teach
Your example was our instructor
Of the respect a dignified life achieves

Dear dad, you've simply cared for us
Through good and bad...a lifetime through
You'll never know the depths of our love
And our heartfelt gratitude

We'll be forever thankful for all that you did
For showing us what a good man should be
You were the greatest hero to us
The best Dad that there could be!

A Man Who Loved His Family

Our Dad was one of those special men
Who truly knew what life was about
Who demonstrated that his family came first
For his actions left no room for doubt

Our Father's greatest joy was his children
In fact, there was no faster way
To light up his face with an ear-to-ear smile
Than the mention of his own children's names

He preferred to discuss his children's accomplishments
Rather than his own
And loved to recall the sweet memories
Of his young children and how they had grown

He was a Father who often tucked us in bed
Told bedtime stories, then turned out the light
Reassuring us that he'd always be nearby
If we ever needed him at night

A Father who loved to be near us
Who took us on family vacations
The rock of strength we came to rely on
Through the challenges and trials life gave us

Which doesn't mean to imply that Dad didn't appreciate
The finer things that life can bring
Only that he considered his family's happiness
The best fulfillment of his life's efforts and dreams

And we understood how blessed we were
To have this type of Dad
A Father who cared for us above all else
Willing to give us all he had

A Man Who Loved His Family (Continued)

—

There are many things that could be said about Dad
For he was a man of goodness, honor and trust
But anyone who knew Dad would also remark
On the deep and committed love he felt for us

So as we say goodbye and we remember
Alt. Verse: So as we pause to remember
Our Father's life...the man he came to be
He'd be happiest being remembered by all who knew him
As a man who loved his family

YOUR DREAMS WERE ALL FOR US DAD

YOUR DREAMS WERE ALL FOR US DAD, ALL FOR US
YOU TRADED YOUR OWN DREAMS TO PURCHASE OURS
WILLING TO ACCEPT LESSER OPPORTUNITIES
SO THAT WE WOULD HAVE EVERY OPPORTUNITY

EVERY POSSIBILITY
EVERY CHANCE FOR A GOOD EDUCATION
EVERY SECURITY AND CONFIDENCE
EVERYTHING!

AND OUR DREAMS BECAME YOUR HOPES AND ASPIRATIONS
WE KNEW THAT WE WERE NEVER ALONE IN OUR DREAMS
FOR YOU WERE RIGHT THERE WITH US

YOU DIDN'T MIND IF YOU DIDN'T GET THE BEST EDUCATION
AS LONG AS WE WERE AFFORDED THAT OPPORTUNITY
IT DIDN'T MATTER IF YOUR WORK WASN'T WHAT YOU HAD HOPED FOR
AS LONG AS IT GAVE US THE MEANS TO CREATE OUR OWN FUTURES

YOU WILLINGLY ACCEPTED ALL THOSE HOURS AWAY FROM US
WORKING LONG AND HARD
YOU WERE OKAY WITH IT...
AS LONG AS IT PROVIDED YOUR FAMILY WITH SECURITY AND STABILITY
SO WE GREW UP SURROUNDED IN YOUR DEEP LOVE AND IN YOUR SAFETY
YOU PROVIDED THE ROOM IN OUR HEARTS FOR IMAGINATION TO GROW
YOU TOOK CARE OF THE WORRIES
SO THAT OUR HEARTS AND MINDS COULD PURSUE OUR DREAMS

YOU NEVER SPENT MUCH ON YOURSELF
YOU NEVER ENJOYED MANY OF THE FINER THINGS IN LIFE
WE WERE THE TREASURE YOU INVESTED YOUR LIFE IN
AND YOU GAVE EVERYTHING YOU HAD FOR US
EVERYTHING DAD!
EVERYTHING!

Your Dreams Were All For Us Dad

And now we have lives that are abundant and full
Blessed with rich memories and cherished opportunities
We are surrounded in the peace and love of family
And trusted, loyal friends

We have a life that was paid for in advance
Through the difficult and dedicated efforts of a loving father
Who traded the best years of his own life
To make sure we'd have the best years of ours

Dad, you will never be forgotten!
Your love and sacrifice will never leave us
We will never question our own true worth
For you proved our value to us every single day

And now we hope that our lives have rewarded <u>your</u> dreams
Satisfied every dedicated effort you gave for us
Given you every honor
Every sense of pride
Every happiness and peace
Every dream fulfilled
Everything!

You and your cherished legacy will live on forever
In the lives and hearts of your family
For you have truly purchased a better life for all of us
Through everything that you willingly sacrificed
You gave us everything Dad!
Everything!

Too Rough For Heaven

Dear Lord, we think a mistake's been made
And we feel it's right and proper
To inform you of this error made
And ask you to consider our offer

You see...you took someone from us
Who's too rough around the edges
And would be better off on earth with us
Than up with you in heaven

And it wouldn't be a hardship
For us to take him back
Just send him back to us...safe and sound
And there'll be no questions asked

We're even prepared to list the reasons
That he'd be better off right here
And we're sure when they're considered
Your choice will be quite clear

He's just not ready for heaven yet
Right now he'd find it quite a task
But if you'll give him a few more years
We'll work on fixing that

First, you'll find he prefers a pair of jeans
And well-worn shoes or boots
To whatever it is that you wear up in heaven
Be it robes or business suits

For he's much too hard a worker
To keep clothes pristine...he'd make a fuss!
And though you need hard workers in heaven
He'd still be better off with us

Second, when you consider
The language for which he's known
His colorful words would shock the angels
So you might want to send him home

Too Rough For Heaven (Continued)

For though you'd respect that he speaks the truth
And "says things as they are"
Frankly, we need more truth like his here on earth
Heaven is just too far

He doesn't have perfect table manners
He prefers beer to a glass of wine
He's just not ready for your heavenly feasts
His manners aren't that refined

And we realize you appreciate his kindness
And the respect he's rightly earned
From those of us privileged to know him
But it's one more reason he should be returned

Yes...his family knows his heart of gold
And you're right...there never existed a truer friend
Okay...we can see why you want him up in heaven
But he's someone, upon which, we depend

And so we, his family and dearest friends
Are asking you to change your mind
Give us a few more years with him
And we'll smooth his rough edges over time

And you may feel he's already ready
To be with you forever
Yet even knowing his goodness
We can't bear to lose him either

So give us a decade...or two...more with him
That's all we simply ask
Please return him to his family and friends
For we'll gladly take him back!

How Do I Say Goodbye To A Brother Like You?

How do I say goodbye to a brother
That I love as much as you?
I still cannot believe you're gone
I'm still hoping it isn't true

Wishing this heartache was just a dream
From which I'd wake up and find
You still here, in life, with us
Or if not...somehow time we could rewind

For I don't know how to do it
How to say goodbye to a brother like you
There's almost no one who's shared so much of my life
Who knows me as well as you

I often think upon the mem'ries we shared
When we were very young
You teased me, played with me, and laughed with me
When our lives had just begun

When we shared simple thoughts and simple dreams
And were lost in childhood's plans
Dreaming up our next adventures
In the vivid ways only children can

And as we grew up, there were more special moments
That proved the depth of your love and care
As you helped me through difficult moments
When I needed you...you were always there

My life has been guided and truly blessed
In so many ways by your loving soul
And I'll miss you more than I could ever say
Or that you could ever know

Still the feeble words need expression
Declaring my heartfelt gratitude
Acknowledging all that you meant to me
And my endless love for you

My Sister And My Friend

Sisterhood is a journey
Throughout life it does not end
But you were more than my sister
I was proud to call you my friend

In our childhood, I recall so many times
Of great joy and carefree play
Memories that comfort and make me smile
Even though you've gone away

And I realize how very blessed I was
To have found a friend in you
There were times when your love was the difference
That somehow got me through

Through the challenges that we all must face
Growing up on this path called life
You were there for me in such thoughtful ways
And helped me through these difficult times

And I was also privileged to laugh with you
My mem'ries range from the ridiculous to the sublime
Your smile is seared in my memory
And it will not fade with time

—

I am so grateful that you were my sister
That we journeyed through this life together
And I know it's a bond that will not end
That it will link our souls forever

And even though you've moved on to heaven now
My appreciation will never end
Truly, I was privileged to call you my sister
And even more blessed to call you my friend

Our Twin Hearts Once Beat Together

We shared everything between us
A special sibling trust
Conceived in love together
By parents destined for us

Who waited for us daily
Gratefully praising God above
Anticipating our tiny footprints
Our sloppy kisses and baby hugs

Whose love grew deeply tender
While daily we changed and grew
Who dreamed the dreams of all we'd be
As parents always do

While our hearts beat close together
And we touched each other's faces
Twisted and turned as we played together
In this warmest and safest of places

Growing there we didn't know
Our time together would be so brief
That our births would usher in equal parts
Of inexpressible joy and heart-breaking grief

For life is such a fragile thing
And for us, this couldn't be more true
For it was life and death's struggle that separated us
You from me, and I from you

Yet I fought as hard and bravely
As my body would allow
But God had other plans for me
And I'm with Him in heaven now

Our Twin Hearts Once Beat Together (Continued)

So you will grow up knowing
You were part of a special bond
Two hearts that beat together
Till I left for heaven's beyond

—

Please know that I'll be watching over you
From my place in heaven above
Proudly seeing all the ways you'll grow
Forever sending you my love

So make sure to go to the park for me
And build sand castles on the beach
And I will smile seeing the fun you'll have
With life's adventures... just beyond my reach

Please be happy as you grow each day
Give Dad and Mom extra long hugs for me
Know that I'll miss you all, until it's time
For each of you to return to me

And when you blow out your birthday candles
I will be there too
In fact, I'll never be too far away
I'll daily watch over you

—

So always remember that you are one of two
Whose hearts once beat together
For our bond of love is an eternal one
And it will carry on forever

Sleep Our Little Angel

Sleep our Little Angel
Here so briefly...
Our bright light
The sunshine of our hearts

Play our Little Angel
Up in Heaven
There'll be no skinned knees
And no more tear-filled eyes for you

Instead, you'll dance with the angels
Filling the heavens with your laughter
And we will listen closely...to hear it in our hearts

You brought us so much meaning
From the moment we knew you were coming
You have filled us with happiness
And we never realized
We could feel so complete

You brought us so many smiles
And they still come...
Whenever we think of you
You were PURE JOY!

Stay close our Little Angel
We'll be with you again some day
Don't be sad when we cry for you...
Just pat our tears with your sweet little hands
And warm our face with your brightest smile
And we will feel it...and know that you are near

SLEEP OUR LITTLE ANGEL (CONTINUED)

SO DEAR SWEET ANGEL
SING YOUR SONGS
AND LAUGH YOUR LAUGHTER
AND TUMBLE THROUGH THE CLOUDS
AND DANCE WITH THE ANGELS

AND KEEP OUR LOVE FOR YOU
BUNDLED TIGHTLY IN YOUR HEART
WE WILL DO THE SAME 'TIL THAT HAPPY DAY
WHEN WE'LL HOLD YOU AGAIN...
FOREVER IN OUR ARMS

REMEMBERING YOU WITH GLADNESS

WHEN YOU WERE BORN, ON THAT SPECIAL DAY
I HELD YOU CLOSE TO ME
AND JOY OVERFLOWED FROM DEEP IN MY HEART
WITH A POWER I'D NEVER CONCEIVED

AND I KNEW FROM THAT VERY MOMENT
THAT YOU WERE A GIFT OF LOVE
SENT TO BLESS MY LIFE IN SO MANY WAYS
TRULY SENT FROM GOD ABOVE

WATCHING YOU GROW WAS A PRIVILEGE
DAILY MARVELING AT THE CHANGES IN YOU
FINDING IT HARD TO CONTAIN MY EXCITEMENT
DREAMING OF ALL THE FUTURE THINGS WE'D DO

BOTH WANTING TIME TO SLOW DOWN AND SPEED UP
SOMETIMES WISHING A BABY YOU COULD STAY
OTHER TIMES, WISHING THE YEARS COULD MOVE FASTER
PERHAPS IN MY OWN SELFISH WAY

FOR I HAD SO MANY THINGS TO SHOW YOU
THINGS PLANNED FOR US TO DO AND SEE
WANTING TO GIVE YOU EVERY EXPERIENCE
THAT A MAGICAL CHILDHOOD WOULD NEED

AND I LOVED ALL THE THINGS WE DID TOGETHER
TO HAVE YOUR SWEET SHADOW FOLLOWING ME
I SWELLED WITH PRIDE WHEN YOU CALLED ME "DADDY"
ALT. VERSE: I SWELLED WITH PRIDE WHEN YOU CALLED ME "MOMMY"
BEING YOUR FATHER MEANT SO MUCH TO ME
ALT. VERSE: BEING YOUR MOTHER MEANT SO MUCH TO ME

Remembering You With Gladness (Continued)

Words couldn't express my joy at your birth
And will never express the loss in my heart
Knowing you've left and returned to heaven
That it was deemed your time to part

And though I'm not sure how I'll get through this grief
I promise this much, my dearest son to you
Alt. Verse: I promise this much, my dearest daughter to you
That I'll remember you each day with gladness
For that is what you'd want me to do

And though such deep sorrow cannot be wished away
It isn't the memory you'd want to leave
No, you'd want me to remember you with gladness
Cherishing all the joys you brought to me

So I'll remember all the special times
And I'll treasure every single day
Filled with moments both planned and unexpected
When I was blessed with your loving gaze

And I'll remember your smiles and laughter
And I'll cherish every tender hug
That your little arms could give me
Though I could never have enough!

And I'll long for the day when I'll see you again
When I'll see your sweet smile light up your face
And 'til then, I'll remember you with deepest gladness
That even grief and sorrow cannot erase

You Were The Pride Of Our Hearts

It's so difficult to let you go
Though death's left us no other choice
We're mourning the loss of never seeing you again
Of never hearing your precious voice

It seems that in life there are certain times
Which are more than "simply unfair"
When our hearts search out for better answers
But cannot seem to find them there

And such is the case at your passing
Contemplating the briefness of your life
All the great things that you still would have done
If you'd been granted a little more time

It isn't difficult to envision the possibilities
For look at what you'd already done
The difference you'd made in so many lives
In all that you had become

Perhaps you were simply too good for this life
So God called you back to Heaven
That your life needed no further testament
Than the goodness you'd already given

But regardless of the reason
For why you had to depart
We will miss you every single day of our lives
For you were the pride of our hearts!

Thank you for being our example
Inspiring us through your courage and drive
We'll cherish all the precious memories
That you lovingly created in our lives

<u>You Were The Pride Of Our Hearts (Continued)</u>

For truly your life reflected
A wisdom that few, so young, can see
Yet your humbleness kept you from realizing
The legacy your life would leave

Still we'll miss you most for your love and your smiles
For they made our world seem so bright
And we'll treasure each memory and moment
Every way you blessed our pathways in life

And though we can't quite understand
Why so soon you had to part
We're eternally grateful for the gift of your life
You were truly the pride of our hearts!

GONE TOO SOON

(LOVED ONE'S NAME), WE WEREN'T PREPARED FOR YOU TO GO
YOU WERE TOO FULL OF LIFE TO BE
TAKEN AWAY FROM US SO SOON
IT'S STILL HARD TO BELIEVE

HOW MUCH WE'LL MISS YOUR SMILE
AND YOUR LAUGHTER IN OUR EARS
YOUR ABSENCE LEAVES A HOLE IN US
WE'RE FILLING WITH OUR TEARS

YOU TAUGHT US HOW TO BE OUR BEST
TO IN THE MOMENT LIVE
TO NEVER HOLD A GRUDGE FOR LONG
AND LOYAL FRIENDSHIP GIVE

YOUR PRESENCE WAS A LIGHT AND JOY
WE NEVER REALIZED WOULD SOMEDAY END
JUST LIKE THE BRILLIANT FALLING STAR
THAT CURVED 'ROUND HEAVEN'S BEND

AND THOUGH WE CANNOT UNDERSTAND
THE REASONS GOD TOOK YOU NOW
WE'LL DO OUR BEST TO ACCEPT THIS LOSS
TO CARRY ON SOMEHOW...

—

(LOVED ONE'S NAME), WE CAN'T BEAR TO SAY GOODBYE
BUT YOU WOULDN'T WANT US MOURNING IN DISTRESS
SO WE'LL SMILE THROUGH THESE FALLING TEARS
COUNTING OUR TIME WITH YOU QUITE BLESSED

WE WILL REMEMBER YOU FOREVER
FOR YOU, OUR HEARTS WILL ALWAYS HAVE ROOM
WE LOVED YOU MORE THAN YOU WILL EVER KNOW
YOU LEFT US WAY TOO SOON!

You Were Taken On Angels' Wings

* Note: This is a funeral poem about SIDS (Sudden Infant Death Syndrome)

You were taken on angel's wings
As you sweetly and quietly slept
And returned to heaven before we knew
That you had even left

Our hearts are heavy and sorrowed
That our time with you was so brief
For you were our gift of heaven's light
That is now replaced with grief

But not so much that we won't be grateful
For every second that you were here
You filled our hearts with so much joy
Treasured memories we'll hold forever dear

And though we weren't blessed to see you grow up
We were blessed to see you smile
And to hold you lovingly in our arms
For just a little while

Even though you're in heaven now
We trust you're not too far away
To be close to us when we long for you near
For a part of our family you'll always stay

We'll look forward to the day when you're with us again
When the happiness that has left us will never again part
For when you left on angel's wings
You took with you the deepest love in our hearts

Brave Warrior

Before this world had started
Before our lives began
God assigned us all our challenges
Some hard things to withstand

Each of us were given
Some difficult things to do
But God gave his bravest warriors
An extra burden too

So you came to this earth in a body
Alt. Verse: So you were challenged with a body
Broken and quite ill
Alt. Verse: That became broken and quite ill
But life could never take from you
A solid, determined will

You kept your face turned toward the sunshine
Trapped in a body that only knew rain
And chose to see the joys in life
In spite of constant pain

And though your body was oft' connected
To needles, machines and tubes
You bravely faced each day with them
While expressing gratitude

For the chance of simply being here
Though to us it didn't seem fair
To see someone as special as you
Suffer in a body beyond repair

So when you'd honorably completed
Every trial you were assigned
God chose to bring you back to him
Freeing your bright spirit and mind

Brave Warrior (Continued)

And though we'll miss you deeply
So cherished and loved were you
We know you're enjoying the freedom of heaven
Enjoying things that here you couldn't do

And we are certain God is happy
To have you in Heaven again
To have His brave and loving child
Close and safe with Him

We know you'll continue to watch over us
For it's something you've always done
And that you'll never be too far from us
In the days and years to come

—

So (Loved One's Name), sweet dreams for now...
Peacefully may you rest...
Confident in all the hearts you touched
And in all the lives you blessed

We do not doubt we'll see you again
Someday whole and completely healed
For (Loved One's Name)...
you were one of the bravest warriors
To ever grace life's battlefield!

THE VALIANT FIGHT

THE VALIANT FIGHT IS NOT QUICK, NOR EASY
'TIS A STRUGGLE OF ARDUOUS LENGTH
IN WHICH FEW HAVE BATTLED MORE NOBLY
FOUGHT WITH MORE COURAGE OR STRENGTH

REFUSING TO ACCEPT THE PROBABILITIES AND ODDS
ODDS THAT COUNTED THEM AN EASY PREY
STRIVING TO REMAIN WITH CHERISHED LOVED ONES
DETERMINED THEY'D SOMEHOW FIND A WAY

BRAVELY ENDURING PAIN AND WEAKNESS
IN EXCHANGE FOR THE CHANCE IT WCULD PROVIDE
TO GIVE THEIR BODY MORE TIME TO FIGHT THE BATTLE
HOPING FOR A HEALING OVER TIME

GIVING THEIR BEST THROUGH ALL THE CHALLENGES
PUSHING THEIR BODY PAST THE LIMITS OF ITS STRENGTH
TOUCHING THE HEARTS OF ALL WHO WITNESSED
THIS BATTLE OVER UNEXPECTED LENGTHS

...AND FOR A TIME EVEN DEATH ITSELF
TURNED AND HUNG ITS HEAD IN SHAME
SUBDUED BY THE COURAGE AND VALIANT STRENGTH IT SAW
IN THE SOUL IT SOUGHT TO CLAIM...

YET ETERNITY'S PURPOSES MAY DIFFER
FROM OURS IN THIS EARTHLY FRAME
AND AT TIMES DEATH'S REBIRTH TO LIFE ETERNAL
ACCOMPLISHES PURPOSES WE'RE UNABLE TO EXPLAIN

SO THERE ARE TIMES WHEN DEATH IS ALLOWED
TO TAKE A SOUL FIGHTING THE VALIANT FIGHT
YET (LOVED ONE'S NAME)'S BRAVERY WASN'T DIMINISHED
BECAUSE THE OUTCOME WAS DEATH, INSTEAD OF LIFE

THE VALIANT FIGHT

AND THOUGH <u>HIS/HER</u> LOSS IS TRULY TRAGIC
AND <u>HIS/HER</u> ABSENCE SO VIVID AND STRONG
OUR HEARTS SWELL WITH PRIDE, HAVING WITNESSED <u>HIS/HER</u> BRAVERY
THE LEGACY OF COURAGE TO WHICH <u>HE/SHE</u> BELONGS

AND OUR FINAL FAREWELLS WERE EXEMPT OF ANY REGRETS
ONLY MARKED BY ADMIRATION AND DEEPEST LOVE
A LOVE THAT WILL CARRY US THROUGH 'TIL THAT BLESSED DAY
WHEN WE ARE REUNITED IN HEAVEN ABOVE

Did You Know How Much We Loved You?

*Note: This is a funeral poem for a suicide.

Did you know how much we loved you?
With our whole hearts!

We have to believe that had you truly known...
You never would have chosen this path
That our love would have sustained you

That it would have shone a light in the darkness
To help you find your way home
Back to peace with your life
To peace with yourself
And also back to us

The heartache we feel is as strong as our love for you
Both are so deep, they'll be never-ending

And our regret is
that we might not have been able to express this love
In such a way that you absolutely knew it
And never doubted it
In a way that gave you strength,
Comforted your heart,
And helped you through your challenges

Sadly, time can't be turned back
Though we'd give anything to make it so
We can only hope that you are now at peace

—

Did You Know How Much We Loved You?

But just in case you're listening...
We loved you from the moment that we knew you were coming to us
Alt. Verse: We loved you from the moment we met you
We love the memories of your life with us
We loved your laughter and your smile
We loved all the ways you blessed our lives
We loved you...just for being you

May our love comfort and surround you until we meet again...

We love you (Loved One's Name)
We love you!

Broken Heart

*Note: This is a funeral poem for a suicide.

I know the way I left you
Wasn't the easiest way to leave
I'm sorry I couldn't have made it easier
Somehow lessened all the grief

But you see I have been struggling
For some time with a broken heart
And my best efforts to repair it
Couldn't begin to start

To take away the pain I felt
To help me feel some hope
My spirit was daily dying
And I lost the strength to cope

I know you had no notice
But how could I begin to say
That I couldn't keep on just existing
Surviving day by day?

You would have begged me to continue trying
You would have done most anything
It might have worked...but maybe not
To heal this wound in me

So don't be caught up in worry
Never think to blame yourselves
For I've gone to God who is over All
Seeking the One True source of help

Know that I'll love you forever
And can't wait for you to see
The wondrous gift of healing
God is fashioning in me

Broken Heart (Continued)

And there may be some who feel my choice
Is a selfish evil sin
But I know that God understands my pain
And I'll be judged by only him

So in the midst of such deep sadness
Feel some happiness too for me
For God's now healing my broken heart
And He's setting my spirit free

You Took A Risk And The Risk Took You

You took a risk and the risk took you
And it breaks our hearts to know
That you've been taken away from us
That you won't be coming home

For in the daring, perhaps some say foolish, act
There was a risk, a chance it would be
The final act to your wonderful life
Though it's still hard to believe

For of the many who'll risk...then survive
There are always a few who'll pay
The ultimate price we understand it might cost
If the odds don't go their way

So your passing will be remembered
With poignant sadness, understanding the cost
That a risk extracted from you and from us
Of dreams denied, of regret, and of loss

But even the sadness can't replace the joy
That you brought into our souls
For you filled our lives with laughter and smiles
Cherished remembrances we'll forever hold

Until the day when we see you again
When you'll wipe the tears from our faces
In a place of beauty that sadness cannot go
Surrounded by God's mercies and His graces

Till then we'll remember you fondly...and with smiles
Grateful for every instant you were here
And loving you with a devotion only reserved
For those we hold most precious and dear

The Hero's Path

You risked your life for others
Each and every day
Understanding and accepting the potential cost
That someday you might pay

For such is the path of a Hero
A terrain where only the brave would choose to go
For 'tis like a mountain pass, narrow and rugged
Far removed from the peaceful valley down below

Yet you walked that difficult path daily
Seeing harsh things, while doing such good
And we loved and respected your courage
More than you understood

And you were a blessing to countless people
Through your selfless and courageous deeds
And you comforted many worried spirits
A guardian angel in their hour of need

Now, you might want to dispute the honor
In fact...it's a title you'd quickly dismiss
But every day you earned it
In the way you chose to live

Your efforts will impact generations
Through lives blessed, and all the good you did
Truly...you were our Hero
And we all thank God that you lived!

A Soldier's Honor

Our lives are built upon a framework
The framework of privilege and freedom
Purchased through the blood, sweat and tears
Of our soldiers, those brave men and women

A soldier's heart has known courage
For they've placed liberty before their own life
And they're well acquainted with dedication
Protecting the rights due mankind

Leaving the comfort and safety of loved ones
Committing to a high and noble purpose
Blessing nations and people they've never before met
Giving them a taste of peace's hopeful assurance

Loving freedom and understanding its power
Being a symbol of that hope in the world
Accepting the possibility that fate may require
Their ultimate sacrifice to propel freedom forward

A soldier's honor fills their family with pride
Though the pain of their absence is ne'r far away
And a soldier's honor extends to their family
As they bear this lonely sacrifice day-by-day

A soldier serving in a brotherhood and sisterhood of arms
Bonded together as a "second family"
Worrying and watching over buddies in this life
And in death, mourning them with deepest grief

And whether a soldier sees the results of their efforts
Fulfilled across a lifetime fully lived
Or whether they're taken, in an instant, back to God
When they still had so much good in them to give

A Soldier's Honor (Continued)

When an honorable soldier leaves this earth
They take their rightful place in Heaven
Having earned this mighty reward
Through the selfless service they've given

And a soldier's honor doesn't end with their death
It becomes a lasting legacy
As future generations are blessed by their efforts
Their willingness to pay the necessary price for peace

I Lost Myself When I Lost You

I lost myself when I lost you
And I cannot seem to find
The life I had before you left
Before hopelessness conquered my mind

People tell me it will get better
And perhaps in time it will
But right now, I'm simply existing
Numbly trying to feel

Any emotion that extends beyond pain
Any tiny ray of hope
Wishing for a light to guide me through the darkness
Some method or means to cope

And so each day I awaken
And I take the time to breathe
Mechanically going through the motions
With a broken heart that grieves

Yet I'm deeply grateful for sweet mem'ries
Which provide brief moments of respite
And almost help me to accept this loss
Well almost...but not quite

Memories that make me so grateful
That I knew you loved me and I loved you
I think if I focus on these mem'ries
They just might see me through

To the other side of this heartache
Beyond this valley of despair
Guiding me past the step-stones of sorrow
To a future happiness...out there somewhere

I Lost Myself When I Lost You

And so that hope keeps me going
That if I keep trying, I someday might
Find the road to happiness again
And somehow reclaim my life

Yet you will never leave me
You are part of me forever...deep in my soul
And I'll carry your treasured memory with me
Wherever I will go

WHY?

WHY?
WHY DID THIS HAPPEN TO ME?
WHY NOW?
WHY TO SOMEONE I LOVED SO MUCH?

WHY DO I HAVE TO SUFFER LIKE THIS?
WHY DO I HAVE TO SEE OTHERS SUFFERING SO MUCH?
WHY COULDN'T WE ALL HAVE BEEN TAKEN TOGETHER?
IN A BETTER TIME...IN A BETTER WAY...WHEN WE WERE READY
WHY?

WHY CAN'T WE GO BACK AND FIX IT?
OR AT LEAST TRY TO?
WHY DOES IT ALL HAVE TO BE SO FINAL?
WHY?

WHY DOES THIS SUFFERING SEEM SO UNNECESSARY?
SO POINTLESS...SO UNENDING?
WHY?

AND WHY CAN'T WE SEE OUR LOVED ONES ON THE OTHER SIDE?
KNOW WHERE THEY'VE GONE...
WHY ARE WE SUPPOSED TO TAKE THIS ALL ON FAITH?
WHY DO WE HAVE TO WAIT TO SEE THEM AGAIN?
WHY?

PERHAPS THERE ARE LESSONS TO BE LEARNED THROUGH THIS TRIAL...
BUT WHY RIGHT NOW?
WHY ME?
WHY TO THE PEOPLE I LOVE?
WHY?

THE MIDNIGHT HOURS

THE MIDNIGHT HOURS ARE THE WORST...
PEOPLE SHOULD WARN YOU MORE ABOUT THAT
THE HOURS BETWEEN DUSK AND DAWN SEEM LIKE AN ETERNITY
THEY CREEP ON PAINFULLY SLOW...MINUTES STRETCH INTO HOURS...
AND ALL YOU DO IS LIE IN THE DARK AND THINK

YOU'RE EXHAUSTED; YOU'D GIVE ANYTHING TO SLEEP
BUT YOU CAN'T
YOU'RE TORN BETWEEN THE SAD THOUGHTS
THAT CONTINUE TO BREAK YOUR HEART
AND THE HAPPY MEMORIES OF YOUR LOVED ONE LOST

AND YOU THINK OF WHAT YOU COULD HAVE DONE MORE OF...
AND THE THINGS YOU DIDN'T DO ENOUGH OF...
AND THE FUTURE CHANCES NOW GONE...

YOU TOSS AND TURN AND SLEEP FINALLY CLAIMS YOU...
A FEW MINUTES AT A TIME...BUT IT IS NEVER FOR LONG
BECAUSE THE SORROW MOMENTARILY FORGOTTEN
IS RENEWED IN THE PARTIALLY-REFRESHED MIND

THE CYCLE JUST GOES ON AND ON...
THERE'S NO INDICATION WHEN IT'LL END
YES, THE MIDNIGHT HOURS ARE THE HARDEST
MOURNING A LOVED ONE AND FRIEND

SAVED FROM THE LONELY SEA

There are times when life is easy
Days pass under sun-filled sky
When sadness is a distant thought
That rarely passes by

Yet other times we're overcome
By waves of cruelty
Sadness and grief wash over us
In a dark and lonely sea

Facing hard things we cannot escape
We are left only to decide
Whether to seek help from God
Or struggle alone in churning tide

For some of us, it is hard to cry out
To a Being we've hardly known
Why would the Lord, Jesus Christ, help us
Who believed we could handle things alone?

And even if we wanted to...
Ask the Lord to come to our side
For some, we are angry God didn't stop the waves
Didn't use His Power to rebuke the tide

And for others, it's just difficult
For us to have faith to believe
That the Lord can actually bind up our hearts
Heal our deepest wounds that bleed

But in our moments of dark, lonely pain
If we'll just ask Him to see us through
In the very moment that we call upon God
That's what he begins to do

Saved From The Lonely Sea (Continued)

He quickly sends us the Holy Ghost
The Comforter streams light in the dark
At times, it's just tiny flutters of hope
Other times, waves of peace flood through our heart

And once we begin to understand
That we can truly trust in Him
We give up defenses of anger and pride
And we fully invite Him in

And as we allow ourselves to be led by the Lord
He shows us the lessons to learn
And helps us navigate the waves of grief
While bypassing despair's crashing churn

And we know He is helping us
For we feel Him daily by our side
As we move onto higher ground
'Til we've finally escaped the tide

—

Then if we'll choose to continue with Him
He'll guide us a lifetime through
In every experience that comes upon us
For that's what He promised to do

And thankfully someday, when this life is over
We'll dwell with our loved ones in peace
And these trials and heartaches...so painful now
Will then be considered bittersweet

For we'll see how fully they helped us improve
Made our love and compassion more deep
And gave us a chance to trust in the Lord
Who then healed all our heartaches and grief

You Weren't The Easiest Person To Love, But I Loved You Anyway

I think of you often, and with pain
I regretfully confess
Your parting has not healed my wounds
Perhaps time will, but not yet

For your life affected mine so deeply
It matters not if you tried your best
And though I recall some happy times
Much sadness filled the rest

And I'm bewildered that through your passing
A deeper grief has been revealed
Than I ever anticipated feeling
Reminding me I'm far from healed

And I've come to acknowledge this reality
That in spite of all the pain
Though you weren't the easiest person to love
I loved you anyway

—

I hope you are finally being freed
From the demons you faced in life
For your journey here wasn't an easy one
That's a fact I can't deny

And whether others broke you, or you broke yourself
I hope that you're freed from your pain
And I hope that God will free me too
Bring me back to wholeness again

And if sometime in the next life we meet
I hope you are different and new
I might like to meet the better person
That remained guarded and hidden in you

YOU WEREN'T THE EASIEST PERSON TO LOVE, BUT I LOVED YOU ANYWAY (CONTINUED)

'TIL THEN, I HOPE THAT YOU ARE HEALING
MAY YOUR TROUBLED SOUL FINALLY FIND THE PEACE
THAT YOU NEVER SEEMED TO FIND IN THIS LIFE
MAY ALL THE PAIN AROUND YOU FINALLY CEASE

AND THOUGH YOU'LL BE REMEMBERED WITH MIXED FEELINGS
AND IT'S LIKELY SADNESS AND ANGER WILL ALWAYS REMAIN
EVEN THOUGH YOU WEREN'T THE EASIEST PERSON TO LOVE
I LOVED YOU ANYWAY

84

Missing You On Special Days

Dear (Loved One's Name), I miss you every day
Your memory often comes to mind
It's still natural for me to think about you
For my love's never faded with time

And it's hard enough to carry on
Still missing you day-by-day
But the loss becomes almost too profound
At certain moments, on special days

Moments you had the right to be with me
On my birthdays to see me smile
At graduation, when I achieved that goal
Or to walk me down the aisle
Alt. Verse 1: To see me walk down the aisle
Alt. Verse 2: To see my bride walk down the aisle

And though I often feel you near
And know you didn't miss these special days
I still regret never being able to see
That look of pride spread across your face

I'm sad I lost the chance to hug you
To express all that you meant to me
And to honor you during special moments
For all the ways you've helped me to succeed

And I know that there'll be more milestones
More celebrations and occasions to come
When I still won't have you here with me
As life continues on...

Yet I feel the need to express it
To share the longing within my soul
Wishing you were with me on these special days
And missing you more than you could know

I Lay My Burdens At Thy Feet

I come to Thee with heavy heart
To lay my burdens at Thy feet
And ask you to renew my soul
My Savior...Lord...My Prince of Peace

My heart is broken and sorrow-filled
At the loss of one I love
'Tis more than I can bear alone
Without Your help from up above

For the path I thought my life would travel
Has now changed...and the future is obscure
It's too dim ahead and I'm too weak right now
To foresee how I'll possibly endure

Still I'm reminded of Your loving promise
That if I'll lay my burdens at Thy feet
That you will give me both strength and rest
As I daily commune with Thee

For Your power has no limits
Thy compassion knows no end
You bled for my sufferings in Gethsemane
The cruel cross proved You my truest friend

And though such agony is new to me
It is not new to You
And You know how to succor me
How to love and guide me through

So I'll approach Thy Throne of Grace
Having the faith to do my part
To believe in Your sacred promises
That you will fix my broken heart

You Come Back To Me

Though you are gone, every once in a while
You come back to me
And for a moment it's as though you never left
Your closeness overpowers me

And I feel as if I could stretch out my arms
To take your hand in mine
And hold you during these precious moments
Which logic cannot define

Sometimes it happens on the darkest of days
When my courage turns to bitter despair
As I contemplate the lonely years that I must face
Without you being here

...Then at some difficult moment
You reach out and send me a sign
To confirm that you're watching over me
That life will turn out just fine

Other times I feel you at unexpected moments
It's like you are simply "checking in"
Other times your signs flow to me in other ways
As natural as the tide comes rushing in

To me, these are gifts like glistening diamonds
On a shore of commonplace sand
Passed over by oblivious people
Who cannot see them...or hardly understand

But for my eyes, and heart, only
They are prisms that send forth the light
And reinforce the hope that I must carry
To guide me through this difficult time

You Come Back To Me (Continued)

So you help me through my suffering
Occasionally reminding me to see
That death cannot overpower the bonds of love
Every time you come back to me

So come back to me whenever you can
For nothing's as deep as my love for you
And I cherish each time you come back to me
All the peace I receive from you

The Best Things Come In Small Packages

*Note: This is a memorial poem for a pet

They say the best things come in small packages
And you (Pet's Name), were the best
My cherished and most loyal friend
Who filled my life with happiness

From the very day I brought you home
That love settled deep within my heart
You filled my life with laughter and smiles
A joyful blessing from the start

And as treasured gifts mean more over time
You grew more precious to me with age
These years of experiencing life with you
Brought me more joy than I can explain

Your eyes were mirrors, which went straight to your soul
A soul so loyal, kind and true
You watched over me with careful attention
As any best friend would do

And when my days were bad...you never went far
You supported me throughout the day
And when times were good...what happiness you spread!
In your joyful and loving way

(Pet's Name), you are part of my family
And I'll miss you with deepest grief
Only a hope of seeing you again
Brings my heart some measure of peace

THE BEST THINGS COME IN SMALL PACKAGES
(CONTINUED)

YET KNOWING THE DEVOTED SPIRIT IN YOU
I FULLY TRUST THAT YOU WILL BE
WAITING NEARBY WHEN I RETURN HOME
WHEN WE'RE REUNITED IN ETERNITY

—

SO RUN AND PLAY AND BE AT PEACE
LET YOUR SPIRIT ROAM HAPPY AND FREE
DON'T WORRY THAT YOU HAD TO SAY GOODBYE
AND PLEASE DON'T WORRY ABOUT ME

FOR IN THE FUTURE, YOU'LL BE FOREVER BY MY SIDE
WHEN WE MEET TOGETHER AGAIN
YOU'RE THE BEST GIFT THAT I EVER HAD
MY MOST FAITHFUL AND LOVING FRIEND!

The Fleeting Honors Of Men

When a person's life is completed
Their life is weighed and measured
Judged both privately and publicly
By the things they truly treasured

And people consider the milestones
That dot the life they lived
How they spent their time and effort
And the things they said and did

Many a person would be filled with pride
To have lengthy and accomplished lines
Filling their obituary
As they're remembered one last time

A final chance to impress the crowd
To once more fill them with awe
An obituary that reads like a resume
Describing a life nearly without flaw

Yet how often lofty accomplishments
Achieved during a "picture-perfect" life
Sacrifice the things that matter most
And their loved one's pay the price

Placing family and friends in second place
Convincing themselves it's a temporary need
Yet the race they run never seems to end
For there's no satisfying never-ending greed

Then weeks turn into months and years
Till their loved ones lose all belief and trust
In their empty promises that things will "someday" change
Finally accepting that they're not valued enough

The Fleeting Honors Of Men (Continued)

So when all is said and done this person's honors
Are left to dry on a newspaper's page
In black and white their life is lauded
And forgotten by the next issue's day

For the wealth and honors they traded a lifetime for
Are fleeting and soon dissipate
While privately they're mourned for opportunities lost
Regretted most for the love they never gave

—

So remember that the world's honors
Can't take place of a loved one's trust
That wealth, honors and possessions
Should never come before their needs, or their love

For if you want to be remembered
And cherished throughout eternity
Invest your life in those who love you most
Their admiration is the truest honor you can receive

Life Is A Fragile Thing

Life is a fragile thing
And it can change within an instant
Nothing is safe from the effects of change
No person or possession we're given

The only things we can hold forever
Are the memories in our hearts
The loves we share upon this earth
Before it comes our time to part

So choose a pathway that brings you joy
Take time for quiet moments each day
Appreciate the challenges that strengthen your soul
And the blessings God sends your way

Don't let your heart be ruled by anger
It's just not worth the stress
For the tumult will only expand in your heart
And crowd out happiness

Live each day with wonder and gratitude
For the beauty that surrounds you
And share your abundance generously
It'll ensure future blessings will surround you

Meekly accept that life's journey will include
Unexpected, soul-wrenching heartaches
That will bruise your soul and alter the course
You always imagined your life would take

And when that happens you'll have the choice
To embrace hope or hopelessness
You can't avoid grief, but you can refuse to accept
A lonely future of bitterness

LIFE IS A FRAGILE THING (CONTINUED)

So, choose to be grateful for each moment
With the loved ones you've been given
Value time as a precious treasure
Create happiness in the life you live in

Embrace life, with all its challenges and joys
Appreciate the experiences life brings
Most of all...live fully in each single moment
For life is a fragile thing!

3216854

Made in the USA